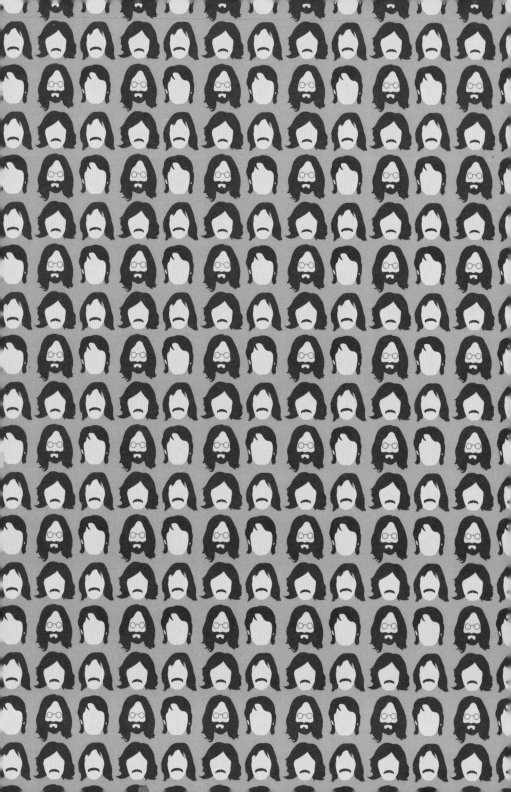

BIOGRAPHIC
THE BEATLES

BIOGRAPHIC
THE BEATLES

VIV CROOT

ILLUSTRATED BY
MATT CARR

AMMONITE
PRESS

First published 2019 by
Ammonite Press
an imprint of Guild of Master Craftsman Publications Ltd
Castle Place, 166 High Street, Lewes, East Sussex, BN7 1XU,
United Kingdom
www.ammonitepress.com

Text © Viv Croot, 2019
Copyright in the Work © GMC Publications Ltd, 2019

ISBN 978 1 78145 369 8

A catalogue record for this book is available from the
British Library.

Publisher: Jason Hook
Concept Design: Matt Carr
Design & Illustration: Matt Carr & Robin Shields
Editor: Jamie Pumfrey

Colour reproduction by GMC Reprographics
Printed and bound in Turkey

CONTENTS

ICONOGRAPHIC

WHEN WE CAN RECOGNIZE A BAND BY A SET OF ICONS, WE CAN ALSO RECOGNIZE HOW COMPLETELY THOSE MUSICIANS AND THEIR MUSIC HAVE ENTERED OUR CULTURE AND OUR CONSCIOUSNESS.

ABBEY
ROAD NW8
CITY OF WESTMINSTER

INTRODUCTION

There is something rather Shakespearean about The Beatles; like him, they too had a way of combining genius with the common touch so that anybody, anywhere, anytime and at any level can appreciate them. According to music critic Richie Unterberger, they were, "Simultaneously the best at what they did and the most popular at what they did," which is a rare combination in any artistic arena. They were phenomenally popular in their own time (Beatlemania was so powerful it became a subject of academic study) and today, almost 50 years since they split up, they are still the bestselling band in history (over 600 million records). And, of course, they changed the world forever.

In 1960s Liverpool, you couldn't throw a guitar pick without hitting a fledgling pop group. The Beatles were just one more quartet (occasional quintet) of ambitious, randy boys. You couldn't say they were an overnight sensation. They paid their dues in the strip joints of Hamburg, Germany, and when they came back to the UK, they played The Cavern Club in Liverpool almost 300 times – as well as many other one-off gigs – before their besotted young manager, Brian Epstein, could get any record company interested in his boys. Decca Records famously turned them down, but Parlophone took them on and they met George Martin, the producer who helped them become the best band in the world.

When 'Love Me Do' came out in October 1962, it hit adolescent ears like a freight train: here were boys singing in an English accent – a northern accent – not some unconvincing knock-off copy of American. The joy and energy that came bursting out of that simple, stripped-down song somehow communicated, at a visceral level, that the 1960s had officially begun. When they followed it with 'Please, Please Me' and 'From Me to You' – which became their first UK number 1 single – you could feel society was shifting.

Other bands also made it. Some stayed together for longer, but they were somehow static, touring forever with their greatest hits. The Beatles were far more than that. They were transformative game-changers. They were a cultural event. Earnest social anthropologists identified them as 'icons of the 1960s counterculture', crediting them with making possible the cultural reassignment of pop music as art. They wrote their own songs, establishing a creative precedent for upcoming bands. They were witty, gritty and working class. They were also the first British rock group to achieve worldwide prominence.

"I SAY IN SPEECHES THAT A PLAUSIBLE MISSION OF ARTISTS IS TO MAKE PEOPLE APPRECIATE BEING ALIVE AT LEAST A LITTLE BIT. I AM THEN ASKED IF I KNOW OF ANY ARTISTS WHO PULLED THAT OFF. I REPLY, 'THE BEATLES DID'."

—Kurt Vonnegut, Jr, US writer, 1997

When forced off the road by the sheer noise and number of fans, The Beatles moved into the studio and immediately started being transformative all over again. They quickly learned to use the studio itself as an instrument, building its potential into the creative process – mixing up genres, experimenting with sound effects, playing with tapes, bringing in whole classical orchestras, incorporating archive snippets and layering sound collages.

While still masters of the three-minute single, they shifted pop's focus on to the album, which gave time and space for experiment, a chance to make a coherent whole rather than just a collection of greatest hits.

In 1967, they gave us *Sergeant Pepper's Lonely Hearts Club Band*, which has to date sold over 32 million copies worldwide. Drama critic Kenneth Tynan called it, "A decisive moment in the history of Western civilization." Everything about it shifted the paradigm. It was an embryo concept album, the concept being the fake band allegedly performing the songs. As much attention was paid to the album cover as the album itself – in fact, the cover was conceived first, designed and illustrated by pop artists Peter Blake and Jann Haworth. It had a gatefold sleeve, decorated inner bags, and all the song lyrics printed on the back of the album. No-one had seen anything like it.

It was not all joyous creativity, obviously. The untimely death of Brian Epstein, the manager who believed in them so much, hit the band hard and had commercial as well as emotional repercussions. Without him the whole Apple Corps business, an ambitious multimedia empire set up by The Beatles, went rotten from the inside, the result of self-indulgence and naiveté. As the band grew up, there were inevitable tensions and ego clashes, especially between John and Paul, who were happiest together when songwriting but unable to stay civil in daily life. John's ill-judged remark about Jesus, misconstrued and blown out of all proportion, also impacted on their US popularity.

When they finally did break our hearts and split up, it was not the end of the story. Although they were never as powerful individually as they were as The Beatles, each of them went off in an interesting new direction, and sent back despatches. The Beatles as an industry did not stop; all of their songs are still available across all possible platforms and sell by the bucketload; films are still being made about them. After Lennon's murder in 1980, the three remaining Beatles worked together on *Anthology* – a triple-album extravaganza of curated archive material celebrating their years together. Paul and Ringo still tour with their respective bands.

The Beatles provided the soundtrack to the 1960s, mirroring the cultural shifts as they happened. They were there for black leather rock and roll in the beginning, and when we turned to peace, love, understanding and altered states, they were there to chronicle it. They wrote the songs. We sung them.

"CHRISTIANITY WILL GO. IT WILL VANISH AND SHRINK... WE'RE MORE POPULAR THAN JESUS NOW. I DON'T KNOW WHICH WILL GO FIRST, ROCK 'N' ROLL OR CHRISTIANITY."

—John Lennon, 1966

THE
BEATLES

01
LIFE

"JOHN WAS THE NE'ER-DO-WELL FATHER, PAUL WAS THE HARD-WORKING MOTHER TRYING TO KEEP EVERYTHING TOGETHER, GEORGE WAS A SLIGHTLY SURLY TEENAGER, AND RINGO WAS THIS HAPPY-GO-LUCKY YOUNG KID WITH HIS MODEL AIRPLANE. THAT'S REALLY HOW IT WAS."

—Ray Connolly, writer and friend, 1969

DAYS IN THE LIFE

The Beatles were all war babies, born during the Second World War into a city which took a terrible battering. Their circumstances were humble or at best very modest and all knew what hard graft was. Winning places at grammar school gave Paul and George a way out, and John was elevated to middle class-dom when he was sent to live with his aunt and uncle after his parents' marriage broke down. Paul's family were the most socially mobile, moving seven times, every time a step up. Ringo was born into one of the poorest areas in the city. However, all of them rescued themselves, each other – and to a certain extent their city – through their music.

JAMES PAUL McCARTNEY

BORN 18 JUNE 1942

- Eldest of 3
- 1 brother, 1 stepsister
- Lost mother in teens

JOHN WINSTON LENNON

BORN 9 OCTOBER 1940

- 2 half-sisters
- Parents split up
- Lost mother in teens

GEORGE HARRISON

BORN 25 FEBRUARY 1943

- Youngest of 4
- 1 sister, 2 brothers

RICHARD STARKEY (RINGO STARR)

BORN 7 JULY 1940

- Only child
- Parents split up

BORN IN THE SAME YEARS AS THE BEATLES:

1940 Smokey Robinson, (19 February), Tom Jones (7 June)

1942 Jimi Hendrix (right, 27 November), Brian Wilson (20 June)

1943 Mick Jagger (26 July), Keith Richards (18 December)

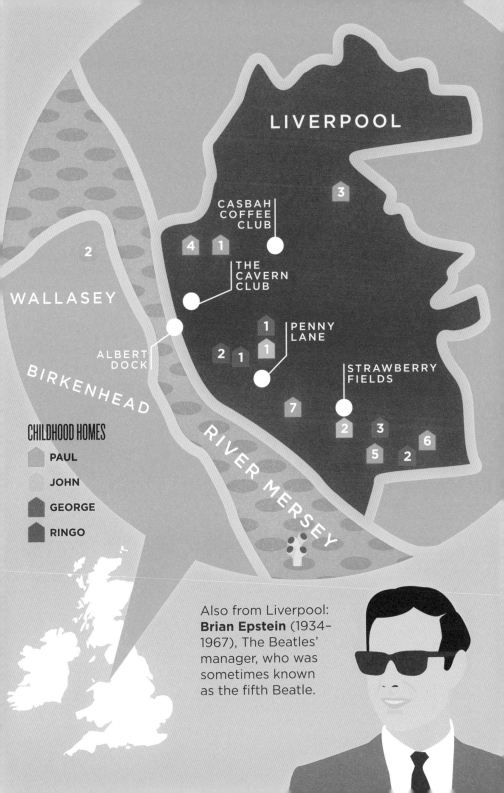

LIVERPOOL

CASBAH
COFFEE
CLUB

THE
CAVERN
CLUB

3

4   1

WALLASEY

2

ALBERT
DOCK

BIRKENHEAD

1   PENNY
         LANE

2   1

1

STRAWBERRY
FIELDS

7

2

2   3

5   2   6

RIVER MERSEY

CHILDHOOD HOMES

PAUL

JOHN

GEORGE

RINGO

Also from Liverpool:
Brian Epstein (1934–
1967), The Beatles'
manager, who was
sometimes known
as the fifth Beatle.

THE NEW YORK OF EUROPE

The American beat poet Allen Ginsberg described Liverpool in the 1960s as, "The centre of consciousness of the human universe." Although his view may be a little hyperbolic, Liverpool has always been a contender. Way back in 1851, *The Banker's Magazine* described it as the New York of Europe. It's a city of firsts, diversity, cultural exchange, ethnic cross currents, confidence, invention – and always looking west across the Atlantic. London may have styled the 1960s, but Liverpool provided the industrial amounts of raw energy that made the decade exciting. It was this raw energy that propelled The Beatles to become – and remain – the most commercially successful pop group in history.

First wet docks in UK

1715

Main emigration point for Europeans to the US (especially the Irish – many of whom never made it, but stayed in Liverpool instead).

People who worked on the boats brought back records and musical styles that were unavailable at home.

THE ROYAL LIVER BUILDING

Designed by Walter Aubrey Thomas to rehouse staff of The Royal Liver Assurance Group, this iconic building of reinforced concrete went up in an astonishing three years, topping out in 1911. On the rooftop, perch two liver birds; if they fly away, legend says the city will crumble.

Home port for Cunard and White Line transatlantic liners

CUNARD

LIVERPOOL POPULATION IN THE 1960s WAS ABOUT 737,000 INCLUDING CITIZENS FROM...

More than **50%** of Liverpudlians have Irish ancestry.

Home to the oldest Chinese community in Europe, dating from the 19th century.

Home of the oldest black African community in the UK, dating from the **1730s**

England

Germany

Ghana

Somalia

Scotland

Italy

Yemen

Wales

Greece

The Caribbean

Ireland

Malaysia

Nordic countries

South Asia

Latin American countries

Ships and people from all over the world coming and going

MERSEY BEAT

Liverpool has always been a key exporter of entertainers – singers, comedians, actors – but in the early 1960s the city diversified big time into rock and pop music. Scouse bands swept the nation and, in The Beatles' case, the world. National media dubbed it 'the Mersey Beat', picking up on the city's influential fortnightly music magazine of the same name, which had been founded by Bill Harry, an art school friend of John's. It was a somewhat incestuous scene, as musicians constantly band-hopped and bands broke up and reconfigured, and it was ferociously competitive. In the early years, The Beatles were just one more bunch of ambitious lads in the Mersey scrum.

Between 1958 and 1964, there were on average 350 Liverpudlian groups playing regular gigs. Here are some of the other bands and artists The Beatles worked with and competed against:

GERRY AND THE PACEMAKERS

BILLY J. KRAMER AND THE DAKOTAS

Billy J was friends with John

RORY STORM AND THE HURRICANES

Ringo was their drummer

CASS AND THE CASANOVAS

THE SCAFFOLD

Mike McGear is Paul's younger brother

DERRY AND THE SENIORS

The Beatles took over from them at the Kaiserkeller

THE VERNONS GIRLS

 The Beatles wrote for them

 Covered/rejected Beatles songs

 Played with/shared stage with The Beatles

THE ESCORTS
Ringo set up a residency for them at The Blue Angel club

THE FOURMOST

THE DENNISONS

JOHNNY GENTLE

BILLY FURY
The Beatles failed the audition to be his backing group

ember of

member of

JOHNNY GUSTAFSON

THE BIG THREE

sang with

KINGSIZE TAYLOR AND THE DOMINOES
Asked Ringo to join the band

CILLA BLACK

sang with

 Other Beatles connection

 Part of the Epstein stable

 Recorded by George Martin

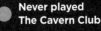 Never played The Cavern Club

 Played in Hamburg

COME TOGETHER!

**Born
9 October.**

Parents separate.

**Attends Mosspits
Primary School,
then Dovedale
Primary.**

**Goes to live with his Aunt
Mimi and Uncle George.
Aunt Mimi is strict but
fair, and John misses
his glamorous,
bohemian mother.**

**Born
18 June.**

**Attends
Stockton
Wood Road
Primary
School.**

**Attends
Joseph
Williams
Junior
School.**

**Born
25 February.**

**Moves to
Speke and
attends
Dovedale
Primary
School.**

**Born
7 July.**

**Parents
split up.**

**Suffers from
appendicitis and
peritonitis, and
takes a year out
of school.**

THE BEATLES

1940 '41 '42 '43 '44 '45 '46 '47 '48 '49 1950 1951

In a city crammed with aspiring rock stars, how did The Beatles find each other and end up with such a successful permutation out of all the possibilities? John and Paul, the nucleus of the band, would probably have met eventually, but they lived in different areas, went to different schools and were two years apart in age so it wasn't guaranteed. If they had not both been at a fete at St Peter's Church in Woolton, and Paul had not been carrying his guitar, and there had been no mutual friend, Ivan Vaughan, to introduce them, The Beatles may never have been. Here's how it all worked out.

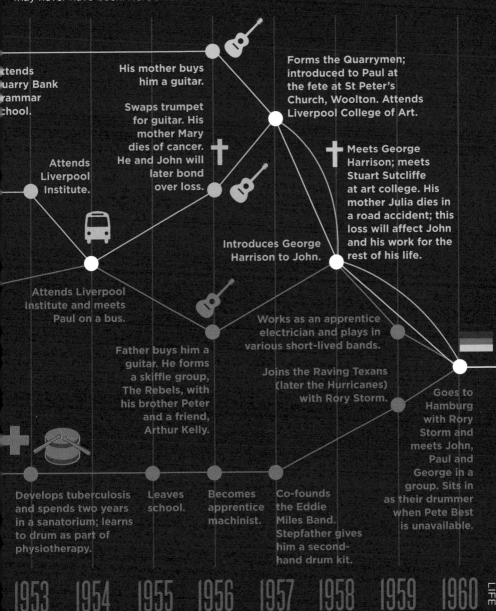

ttends
uarry Bank
rammar
chool.

His mother buys him a guitar.

Forms the Quarrymen; introduced to Paul at the fete at St Peter's Church, Woolton. Attends Liverpool College of Art.

Swaps trumpet for guitar. His mother Mary dies of cancer. He and John will later bond over loss.

Attends Liverpool Institute.

Meets George Harrison; meets Stuart Sutcliffe at art college. His mother Julia dies in a road accident; this loss will affect John and his work for the rest of his life.

Introduces George Harrison to John.

Attends Liverpool Institute and meets Paul on a bus.

Works as an apprentice electrician and plays in various short-lived bands.

Father buys him a guitar. He forms a skiffle group, The Rebels, with his brother Peter and a friend, Arthur Kelly.

Joins the Raving Texans (later the Hurricanes) with Rory Storm.

Goes to Hamburg with Rory Storm and meets John, Paul and George in a group. Sits in as their drummer when Pete Best is unavailable.

Develops tuberculosis and spends two years in a sanatorium; learns to drum as part of physiotherapy.

Leaves school.

Becomes apprentice machinist.

Co-founds the Eddie Miles Band. Stepfather gives him a second-hand drum kit.

1953   1954   1955   1956   1957   1958   1959   1960

BECOMING THE BEATLES

It all began with a skiffle band formed by John in 1956. Very briefly known as The Black Jacks, they were hastily renamed The Quarrymen, John's snarky reference to a line in his school song. After Paul and George joined, the band began to shed its skiffle image (and a few members) and went down the road to rock. They toured briefly in 1959 as Johnny and the Moondogs, but by 1960 they were The Quarrymen once more. They played about with groovier names – The Beatals (Stu Sutcliffe's suggestion), The Silver Beats, The Silver Beetles, The Silver Beatles – and by August 1961 they were officially The Beatles – John, Paul, George, Stu and Pete (Best). Ringo came along later (1962) after back-beating his way through various rock bands, just in time for the group's first hit, 'Love Me Do'.

NOVEMBER 1956

THE BLACK JACKS

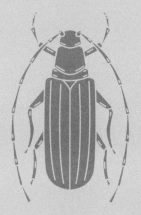

MAY 1960

THE SILVER BEATS

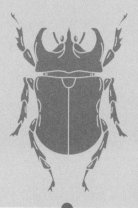

MAY 1960

THE SILVER BEETLES

JULY 1960

THE SILVER BEATLES

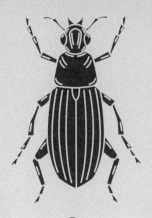

**NOVEMBER 1956-
JANUARY 1960**

THE QUARRYMEN

1956-1959

JOHNNY AND
THE MOONDOGS

JANUARY 1960

THE BEATALS

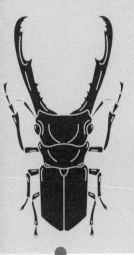

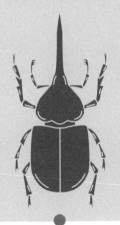

**AUGUST 1960-
DECEMBER 1960**

BEATLES

1961

THE BEAT
BROTHERS

1961 ONWARDS

THE BEATLES

GIVE US A SHOW, LADS!

"Mach Schau!" ("Give us a show, lads!") is what Bruno Koschmider, crippled ex-clown and owner of a very short, grimy string of strip-clubs, used to shout at The Beatles. He had hired them to make some noise and pull in the punters, and this is exactly what they learned to do in the clubs of Hamburg's red-light district. Between 1960 and 1962, The Beatles did five tours of duty in the city, clocking up more than 800 hours on stage. They learned how to really play their instruments, and how to work with each other, work a song and work an audience. Hard graft transformed them from a group of gangly teenage boys into a tight band full of energy, raunch and assured confidence. A class act!

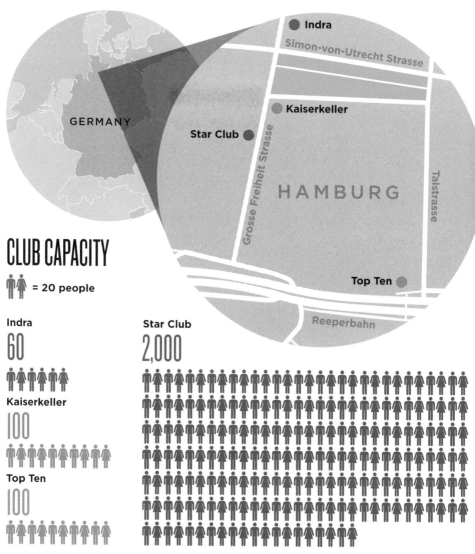

CLUB CAPACITY

👤👤 = 20 people

Indra
60
👤👤👤👤👤👤

Kaiserkeller
100
👤👤👤👤👤👤👤👤

Top Ten
100
👤👤👤👤👤👤👤👤

Star Club
2,000

DATES

INDRA	17 AUGUST TO 2 OCTOBER 1960
KAISERKELLER	3 OCTOBER TO 28 NOVEMBER 1960
TOP TEN	1 APRIL 1961 TO 1 JULY 1961
STAR CLUB	13 APRIL–31 MAY 1962

INDRA

17 AUGUST TO
2 OCTOBER 1960

KAISERKELLER

3 OCTOBER TO
28 NOVEMBER 1960

TOP TEN

1 APRIL 1961 TO 1 JULY 1961

STAR CLUB

13 APRIL–31 MAY 1962

1–14 NOVEMBER 1962

18–31 DECEMBER 1962

TOTAL NIGHTS / HOURS PLAYED

48   56   92   75

217   248   503   260

A HARD DAY'S NIGHT!
(AT THE INDRA AND KAISERKELLER)

7 DAYS A WEEK

4 SETS A DAY

08.30–9.30pm

BREAK

10.00–11.00pm

11.30pm–12.30am

BREAK

01.00–02.00am

5 SETS ON SATURDAY

6 SETS ON SUNDAY

07.00–08.30pm

BREAK

09.00–10.00pm

BREAK

10.30–11.30pm

BREAK

12.00–01.00am

BREAK

01.30–03.00am

05.00–06.00pm

BREAK

06.30–07.30pm

BREAK

08.00–09.00pm

BREAK

09.30–10.30pm

BREAK

11.00pm–12.00am

BREAK

12.30–01.30am

PAY

INDRA AND KAISERKELLER: £2.50 (two pounds 10 shillings) a day each, with ten percent to their agent, Alan Williams.

TOP TEN: £3.00 per day each plus lodgings; no agent fee.

STAR CLUB: between £53 and £67 each per week.

THE FIFTH BEATLE

The Beatles were originally a five-piece band (with Stuart Sutcliffe). When he left in 1961, they did not replace him (Paul took over as bassist) but it became a cultural game to fantasize about who could be called the Fifth Beatle to fill the hypothetical vacant position. Many were put forward for the job, mostly people with a strong personal or musical connection. Not all of them, though. Football legend George Best got the call, despite being neither a scouser, nor a musician, nor an old friend: he did have the haircut, the talent and the chutzpah. Here are some of the most deserving candidates.

STUART SUTCLIFFE
The Real One

Was actually the Fifth Beatle between 1960 and 1961. Not a musician but an inspirational style icon. Left the band to go back to art school before his untimely death in 1962.

PETE BEST
The Unlucky One

Was actually in the band when they were honing their act in Hamburg; played on the first recording of 'Love Me Do'. Sacked in 1962 as his drumming skills and style didn't fit, and was left behind.

BRIAN EPSTEIN
The Managerial One

Recognised the band's talent and raw energy and propelled them along the path to global success; a Beatle in spirit although not in style or background.

ANDY WHITE
The Session One

An accomplished session drummer booked by George Martin. Played on 'Love Me Do' (the third and final recording) and 'P.S. I Love You'.

DEREK TAYLOR
The Press One

A journalist and fan, he worked as Epstein's PA and the band's press officer; understood their approach and humour, and used it to their advantage.

NEIL ASPINALL
The Loyal One

Schoolfriend of Paul and George, became their roadie, chauffeur and general factotum; understood their ways and needs.

THE BEATLES

26

Vocals

 Lead guitar

 Drums

 Bass guitar

 Keyboards

GEORGE MARTIN
The Musical One

Without Martin's musical knowledge and high-end production skills, the band would not have succeeded so well; he allowed them to experiment and fostered their burgeoning talent.

CHAS NEWBY
The Substitute One

Member of Pete Best's first band, The Black Jacks. Replacement bassist for Stuart Sutcliffe for four gigs in Liverpool, December 1960. Turned down the offer to stay on and went back to university.

KLAUS VOORMANN
The Artistic One

Friends with all the band in Hamburg. Played bass with them there after Stuart Sutcliffe left. Designed the album cover artwork for *Revolver*.

JIMMIE NICOL
The Supply One

Stood in for Ringo when he was ill for the first eight shows of the 1964 World Tour: played in Denmark, Netherlands, Hong Kong and Australia.

TONY SHERIDAN
The Lead Singer One

Sang with The Beatles as his backing band in Hamburg; they recorded an album together as Tony Sheridan and the Beat Brothers. Had a hit with 'My Bonnie'.

BILLY PRESTON
The American One

Met in 1962, worked together in 1969. Played occasionally with the band on stage and on the albums *Let it Be* and *Abbey Road*.

ERIC CLAPTON
The Additional Axeman One

Played on 'While My Guitar Gently Weeps', at George's invitation. When George briefly left the band in 1969, John invited Clapton to step in.

THE FAB FOUR!

What made The Beatles 'The Beatles' was the alchemical synthesis of four different personalities. They were so distinct that every fan could have a favourite Beatle, yet worked so well together that they created a glorious whole that was bigger than its individual parts. It's what gave the band a longevity beyond the one-hit wonders and transient pop groups of the day, but what bound them together eventually tore them apart. All things must pass.

JOHN
THE CLEVER ONE

CYNICAL

WITTY

ARTY

SARCASTIC

ARROGANT

REBELLIOUS

DOMINEERING

IDEALISTIC

SECRETLY... INSECURE

PAUL
THE CUTE ONE

CHEERFUL   CHARMING

ENTERTAINING

CO-OPERATIVE

UNCOMPLICATED

SENTIMENTAL   SENSITIVE

APPROACHABLE

AMBITIOUS

GROUP DYNAMICS

- John loved/hated Paul
- Paul loved/hated John
- Paul and George were friends but got on each other's nerves
- John thought of George as an annoying younger brother
- George looked up to John
- Everyone got on with Ringo

GEORGE
THE QUIET ONE

SARDONIC   SILENT

THOUGHTFUL   SPIRITUAL

MUSICALLY ADVENTUROUS

SHY   SENSITIVE

INTROSPECTIVE

HUMANITARIAN

RINGO
THE FUNNY ONE

FUNNY   LAID-BACK

LOVABLE   DOWN-TO-EARTH

UNCOMPLICATED

UNASSUMING

GOOD-NATURED

UNPRETENTIOUS

STUBBORN

SWINGING THROUGH THE SIXTIES

John F. Kennedy wins the US presidency

Berlin Wall erected

Andy Warhol finishes his *Campbell's Soup Cans* piece

John F. Kennedy assassinated

Martin Luther King's "I have a dream" speech

The Beatles invade the US

Civil Rights Act in the US outlaws publi discriminatio

1960

1961

1962

1963

1964

The Beatles play in the Indra club, Hamburg

The US approves use of the contraceptive pill Enovid

À Bout de Souffle – Jean-Luc Godard's New Wave film – is released

Brian Epstein meets The Beatles

The Beatles play their first gig at The Cavern Club in Liverpool

Yuri Gagarin becomes the first man in space

Stuart Sutcliffe dies. Ringo joins the band

ABBEY ROAD NW8
CITY OF WESTMINSTER

The Beatles' first Abbey Road session with George Martin

The Cuban Missile Crisis

The Feminine Mystique by Betty Friedan published

'Please Please Me' released

The audio cassette introduced

Muhammad Ali beats Sonny Liston

The US begin escalation of the Vietnam War

Bob Dylan goes electric at the Newport Folk Festival

JUDAS!

Magically, The Beatles' lifespan fitted the 1960s exactly. What began in a Hamburg cellar in 1960 ended in acrimony in April 1970. The ten years between saw society radically transform from monochrome to full colour in every aspect of life – music, art, fashion, food, literature, sexual mores, civil rights – and the world rocked by events which changed the century, let alone the decade. And The Beatles provided the soundtrack to it all.

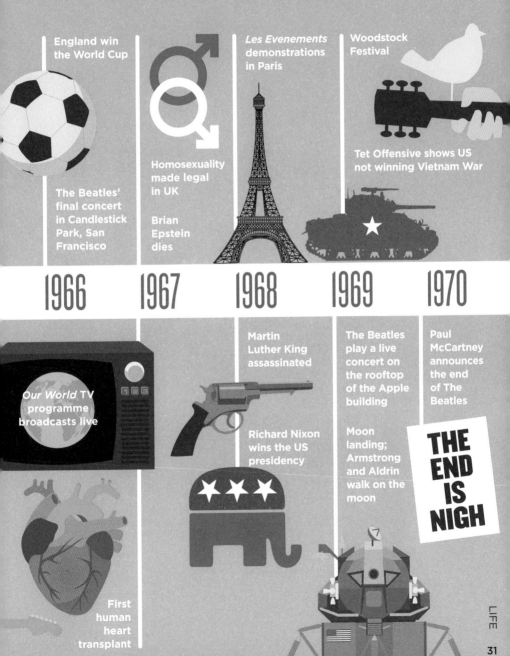

England win the World Cup

The Beatles' final concert in Candlestick Park, San Francisco

Homosexuality made legal in UK

Brian Epstein dies

Les Evenements **demonstrations in Paris**

Woodstock Festival

Tet Offensive shows US not winning Vietnam War

1966 1967 1968 1969 1970

Our World **TV programme broadcasts live**

Martin Luther King assassinated

Richard Nixon wins the US presidency

The Beatles play a live concert on the rooftop of the Apple building

Moon landing; Armstrong and Aldrin walk on the moon

Paul McCartney announces the end of The Beatles

THE END IS NIGH

First human heart transplant

AND IN THE END...

The Beatles finally broke up in 1970, but it had been a cumulative process. Hairline cracks had become gaping fissures by 1968 when many destructive elements coalesced – growing musical differences, distracting solo projects, resentments, jealousies, personality clashes, business problems, drugs and death – making the eventual split inevitable. The decade-long party came to an end. Maybe it was just time.

LET IT BE

1966 Stop touring, and lose that collaborative feeling.

1967 Death of Brian Epstein leaves them rudderless, as a band and a business.

1968 Apple Corps business in a chaotic financial state.

1968 John becomes addicted to heroin.

John involves Yoko in all recording sessions.

George's emerging songwriting talent sidelined by John and Paul.

1968 Others resent Paul appearing to take over managerial duties (while not doing anything themselves).

White Album recording sessions in which everybody is pursuing different agendas, not willing to collaborate, all irritated by each other.

1969 Appointment of Allen Klein as manager.

Members of the band begin to take out lawsuits against one another.

KEY DATES

1968	1969	1969	1970	1975
21 AUGUST Ringo leaves temporarily, returns in September.	**10 JANUARY** George leaves temporarily, returns 15 January.	**20 SEPTEMBER** John decides to leave, but agrees to keep it a secret for business reasons.	**9 APRIL** Paul announces he is leaving.	**9 JANUARY** The partnership of The Beatles is officially dissolved.

THE BEATLES

02
WORLD

"IF YOU
WANT TO
KNOW
ABOUT
The
Sixties

"Play the music of The Beatles."

—Aaron Copland, taken from
*Aaron Copland: The Life and
Work of an Uncommon Man*
by Howard Pollack, 2000

HAMBURG AND HAIRCUTS

Hamburg was not just a rock-and-roll bootcamp for The Beatles, but an adventure in style, philosophy, altered states and sex. While playing at the Kaiserkeller club in 1960, The Beatles met three intrepid 'existentialists' (known as exies) called Klaus Voormann, Astrid Kirchherr and Jürgen Vollmer. Although rockers, the Indra's main clientele, and exies were tribal enemies, the trio dared to penetrate rocker territory to listen to the band. Exies, who based their style on French existential philosophy, were creative, cerebral and cool, and profoundly influenced the band's work and style, introducing them to black leather, intellectual ideas, left-bank haircuts and amphetamines.

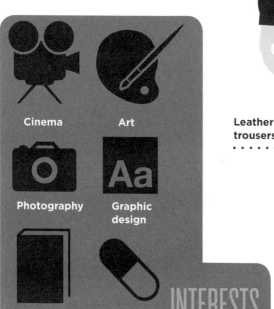

Cinema

Art

Photography

Graphic design

Philosophy/ literature

Drugs

INTERESTS

EXI STYLE:

Long fringe

Polo neck jumper

Collarless jacket

Leather trousers

Black clothes

Black boots

SEX:

Sex education came courtesy of the Reeperbahn, the main artery of Hamburg's red-light district.

REEPERBAHN

HAIRCUTS:

In 1960, Astrid styled Stuart's hair like hers and Jürgen's with a fringe at the front. She had got the idea from a Jean Cocteau movie in 1959.

John and Paul also had theirs done by Jürgen who they met again by chance in the ultra-cool left-bank area of Paris in 1961.

DRUGS:

Preludin®

The Hamburg drugs of choice were amphetamines, called prellies (Preludin), which were then readily available prescription drugs in Germany.

DAILY INTAKE

Paul wasn't keen, and claims he took one pill for every four Stuart and George swallowed – or five in the case of John. Pete Best stuck to beer.

| JOHN | PAUL | GEORGE | STUART SUTCLIFFE | PETE BEST | RINGO NOT YET IN BAND |

The rivalry between The Beatles and The Rolling Stones – north versus south, the lovable Merseyside moptops against the down and dirty kings of the Surrey Delta – was a media fabrication. The hype was all style – The Beatles were framed as the lads next door, and the Stones as the bad boys. But in reality, both bands sprang from the same sort of background at the same time, and shared the same R&B and rock roots and even repertoire. They knew each other and socialized amicably: The Beatles checked out the early Stones in 1963 at the Station Hotel, Richmond, London, and gave them one of their songs ('I Wanna be Your Man'). In fact, the real musical rivals for The Beatles were The Beach Boys.

THE BEATLES

FORMED
1960

BAND UNIFORM

DRUGS

DRUMS   **LEAD GUITAR**   **RHYTHM GUITAR**   **BASS**

4

MEMBERS

SONG WRITING DUO

2 X LEAD SINGERS

GRAMMAR SCHOOL BOYS

GRITTY NORTHERNERS

THE STONES

NUMBER ONES

UK 17   USA 20

13

600 MILLION SOLD

NO BAND UNIFORM

FORMED 1962

YEARS ACTIVE

NUMBER ONES

UK 10   USA 8

23

240 MILLION SOLD

DRUGS

SONG WRITING DUO

10   57

SINGLES 63

5 MEMBERS

DRUMS   LEAD GUITAR   RHYTHM GUITAR

SINGLES 120

BASS

1 X LEAD SINGER

SOFT SOUTHERNERS

GRAMMAR SCHOOL BOYS

WITH A LITTLE HELP FROM MY FRIENDS

No self-respecting band went through the 1960s without indulging in drugs, and The Beatles were no exception. Between them, they tried the lot – speed, weed, marijuana, LSD, heroin and a line or two of cocaine. They were originally advocates for the legalization of cannabis but in August 1967 publicly renounced all drugs, although their abstinence did not last. Drug culture inevitably shaped their music. Some of their late '60s tracks are soaked in trippy atmosphere but hide their meaning; some have overt drug references in the lyrics; and three (or four if you include Lucy in the Sky*) were drug anthems written while under the influence.

HIDDEN HIGHS

'THE MAGICAL MYSTERY TOUR'

'FLYING'

'I AM THE WALRUS'

THE DEEPER YOU GO, THE HIGHER YOU FLY

'WITH A LITTLE HELP FROM MY FRIENDS'

'SHE'S A WOMAN'

'A DAY IN THE LIFE'

'AND YOUR BIRD CAN SING'

'HAPPINESS IS A WARM GUN'

'EVERYBODY'S GOT SOMETHING TO HIDE EXCEPT ME AND MY MONKEY'

'DAY TRIPPER'

HIGH AS A KITE

'SHE SAID, SHE SAID' (LSD)

'TOMORROW NEVER KNOWS' (LSD)

'GOT TO GET YOU INTO MY LIFE'
Paul described this specifically as his paean to pot. (MARIJUANA)

'LUCY IN THE SKY WITH DIAMONDS'*
John always denied a drug connection, and no doubt it was inspired by his son's friend drawing, but those initials and "kaleidoscope eyes"?
Come on... (LSD)

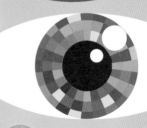

AMPHETAMINES

WHERE: Hamburg clubs

NOT THERE

MARIJUANA

WHERE: The Delmonico Hotel, New York (introduced to it by Bob Dylan)

 FROM 1964

LSD

WHERE: London and Los Angeles

 1965

COCAINE

WHERE: Hamburg and London

1961, 1967–70

HEROIN

WHERE: London (they were offered it on the set of *Help!* in 1965)

1968–69

JOHN   **PAUL**   **GEORGE**   **RINGO**

MAHARISHI MAHESH YOGI

In 1968, burnt out, grieving for the loss of their manager Brian Epstein and running on empty creatively, The Beatles were swept up in the wave of popularity for the teachings of the Maharishi Mahesh Yogi. He had devised Transcendental Meditation, a meditation programme based on Vedic principles but streamlined and tailored to the short attention span of the Western mind. All four went to the Maharishi's ashram in Rishikesh, in the foothills of the Himalayas in India, where they fully immersed themselves, dressing in Indian style and living simply in stone huts. It was not an unqualified success on a spiritual level and ended in acrimony. Creatively, though, it delivered; in their time there and just afterwards, they wrote around 40 songs, including most of the material for *The Beatles* (the *White Album*).

TIMELINE OF EVENTS

24 AUGUST 1967

John, Paul and George with Cynthia (John's wife), Pattie (George's wife), her sister Jenny Boyd, and Jane Asher (Paul's girlfriend) see the Maharishi lecture at the London Hilton.

25–27 AUGUST 1967

All The Beatles and their partners go to Bangor, Wales, for an induction course.

16 FEBRUARY 1968

John, George, Cynthia, Pattie and Jenny arrive in Rishikesh.

1 MARCH 1968

Ringo and Maureen leave.

20 FEBRUARY 1968

Ringo, Paul, Maureen (Ringo's wife) and Jane arrive in Rishikesh.

26 MARCH 1968

Paul and Jane leave.

12 APRIL 1968

John, George, Cynthia, Pattie and Jenny leave.

15 JUNE 1968

The Beatles publicly repudiate the Maharishi, announcing that they had made a 'public mistake'.

HOW MANY DAYS DID THEY SPEND THERE?

RINGO	9
PAUL	36
GEORGE	53
JOHN	53

WHAT IS TRANSCENDENTAL MEDITATION?

Transcendental meditation is a simple, systematic, fast-track meditation programme, based on Hindu tradition but without the suffering and penance. Followers are given a personal mantra to focus their mind and meditate twice a day.

INDUCTION

1. Subjects are taught to meditate over a simple 7-step process.

2. Each subject is given a personal mantra.

3. They learn to use it to meditate for 15–20 minutes twice daily.

WORLD

CLOSE QUARTERS

Although famous for original compositions by John and Paul (and occasionally George), in their early days The Beatles also performed and recorded cover versions of songs by:

Before they had honed their songwriting skills, The Beatles relied on cover versions by artists including Elvis, Buddy Holly and Chuck Berry. As John and Paul developed one of the great songwriting partnerships, the band became a tight-knit, almost hermetically sealed unit, both on stage and in the studio. There was no band-hopping or dramatic flouncing out, and hardly any side hustles. They were a self-sufficient, unbreakable unit until they began to break, at which point collaborations with artists such as Eric Clapton and Billy Preston offered creative escapes for four individuals feeling trapped within the world's most famous group.

6
THE NUMBER OF OTHER MUSICIANS CREDITED ON THE BEATLES' RECORDS

BILLY PRESTON
ANIL BHAGWAT
PETE BEST
TONY SHERIDAN
ALAN CIVIL
GEORGE MARTIN

LARRY WILLIAMS
JOE TURNER
THE TEDDY BEARS
BARRETT STRONG
THE SHIRELLES
CHAN ROMERO
LITTLE RICHARD
ELVIS PRESLEY
CARL PERKINS
BUCK OWENS
THE MIRACLES
THE MARVELETTES
ANN-MARGRET
PEGGY LEE
LITTLE WILLIE JOHN

WHO DID TH

Elvis was a great fan of The Beatles and sang 'Yesterday', 'Hey Jude' and 'Lady Madonna' live on stage.

On the unique occasion when they did collaborate, The Beatles performed with the world...

On 25 June 1967, The Beatles and friends performed their anthemic

'ALL YOU NEED IS LOVE'

to a global audience of...

400 MILLION

on the world's first **LIVE** global televisual link up.

Joining in with them, apart from friends and family and the Liverpool entourage, were Eric Clapton, Donovan, Marianne Faithfull (right), Mick Jagger, Brian Jones, Gary Leeds (from The Walker Brothers), Keith Moon, Graham Nash and Keith Richards.

...EATLES COVER?

RICHIE BARRETT
CHUCK BERRY
JOHNNY BURNETTE
RAY CHARLES
TONY ORLANDO
THE COASTERS
THE COOKIES
ARTHUR CRUDUP
THE DONAYS
LITTLE EVA
THE EVERLY BROTHERS
DR FEELGOOD
EDDIE FONTAINE
BUDDY HOLLY
...Y BROTHERS
...ANDER

Liverpool's original Cavern Club opened in 1957 as a jazz club with aspirations to left-bank cool. It grudgingly accommodated skiffle but spat on rock music. That attitude gradually changed, and by 1960 it had modulated into a beat venue – specifically Mersey beat.

A CELLARFU

The original Cavern Club was formed of three side-by-side barrel tunnels, each about 10ft (3m) wide and 100ft (30m) long, linked by three 6ft (1.8m) arches.

The Cavern Club opened 16 January 1957 and closed March 1973

Paul McCartney played here with The Quarrymen on 24 January 1958

The Beatles played it (with Stuart Sutcliffe and Pete Best) on 9 February 1961

The actual Cavern Club was demolished in 1973 to make way for Merseyrail underground loop. *Sic transit gloria mundi*, you might say. The current reconstructed Cavern Club is a music venue-cum-tourist experience.

F NOISE

The Cavern Club was a glorious, anarchic, unlicensed, smelly sweathole – hot and loud, with great acoustics. Young people rammed into it at lunchtime sessions and in the evenings, just to listen to the music. Between 1961 and 1963, every big-name Liverpool band played there. Brian Epstein turned up to check out The Beatles in November 1961 and was smitten.

Ringo Starr played here on 31 July 1957 with The Eddie Clayton Skiffle Group

John Lennon played here with The Quarrymen on 7 August 1957

The Beatles played The Cavern Club

292

times between 1961 and 1963

COST: 1/3d

For a lunchtime session with The Beatles. That's equivalent to six pence today!

Brian Epstein first saw The Beatles perform here on 9 November 1961 and signed them up

The Beatles played their last gig at The Cavern Club on 3 August 1963

To get into the club, you had to walk down 18 steps, and there were three steps up to the wooden stage.

BEATLE STYLE

EARLY DAYS

The early Beatles' look was defiant and dangerous rock and roll. The leather suits were also a practical choice for the hard graft in Hamburg. Ringo was not with them at the time, and was still in Teddy Boy drapes.

MOD DAYS

Brian Epstein gave them a sharp uniform for touring and public appearances – the collarless Nehru jackets being a nod to the exis. They became corporate – not four individuals but a single entity with a distinctive brand.

The Beatles' fashion style segued from monochrome to full colour, much like the 1960s themselves. Starting out in a dark cellar in their carapaces of black leather, they morphed into mods, with sharp, Italian, mohair stage suits (Epstein wanted them to look smart). Halfway through the decade, they blossomed into colour, dressing in the psychedelic dandyism of the *Sergeant Pepper* period and the mystical hippy comfort of flowing Indian robes. The haircuts followed suit – and so did their fans.

PSYCHEDELIC DAYS

When *Sergeant Pepper* was released in 1967, The Beatles had quit touring. They retreated into the studio and as their musical talent developed, their style began to individuate, and they began to grow apart.

HIPPY DAYS

Also in 1967, they went to India to stay with the Maharishi, and came back in long floaty robes with beads, flowers and flowing locks, which exactly mirrored the hippy style of the Summer of Love. The trip split the band further apart and they started to reclaim their individuality.

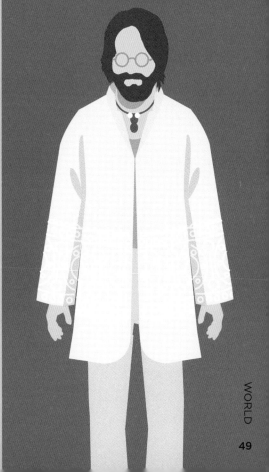

WORLD

BEATLE MANIA!

Orpheus, Franz Liszt, Frank Sinatra, Johnny Ray and Elvis Presley all made the girls sob and faint – but The Beatles made them scream and shout as well. Beatlemania was predominantly a girl thing. Although fuelled by the media, who gave it a name, it was originally a spontaneous eruption, starting on 27 December 1960, when the band – hot from Hamburg – played Litherland Town Hall in Sefton, Liverpool. It was localized at first, but as they began to tour it went nationwide, and by 1964 Beatlemania was an international phenomenon. In the end, it drove the band off the road and into the recording studio. Their last live concert was on 29 August 1966 in Candlestick Park, San Francisco. They couldn't hear themselves play and neither could anyone else.

4,000

Estimated crowd at London Heathrow to watch The Beatles fly off to New York on 7 February 1964 on Pan Am Flight 101. When they arrived home on 22 February they were greeted by a crowd of

10,000

5,000

Estimated crowd when they landed at JFK, New York, plus an additional 200 journalists.

300,000

Estimated crowd in the city centre of Adelaide, South Australia, on 12 June. This was twice as many as turned up to see the Queen in 1963.

ARENA NUMBERS

**Candlestick Park,
San Francisco**

25,000

**Shea Stadium,
New York**

55,000

**Rizal Memorial
Stadium, Manila**

80,000

60db   85db   103db   115db

131db   Sound engineer James Dyble's estimate of the decibel level of the fans and the band combined at the Shea Stadium concert.

NORMAL CONVERSATION

SHOULD WEAR EAR DEFENDERS

JUMBO JET FLYING AT 100 FEET

NORMAL ROCK CONCERT

THE BEATLES' CONCERT AT SHEA STADIUM

SHEA
BASEBALL
STADIUM

APPLE CRUMBLE!

The Beatles set up Apple Corps in April 1967 as an idealistic, co-operative, sybaritic version of a multinational. It was an ambitious multimedia facility – a vehicle to create and publish their own work and that of their friends and any new artists that they liked. (Their accountants saw it as a way of avoiding a potential £3 million tax bill.) Profit was anathema: all profits would be shared equally among the staff, and any left over would be given away. Profligacy, naiveté and self-indulgence quickly demolished most of the dream.

APRIL
Apple Corps is established at 84 Baker Street, London

DECEMBER
Apple Boutique opens at 94 Baker Street

11 MAY
Apple Records launches in the US

30 MAY
The Beatles sta recording the *White Albun*

31 JULY
Apple Boutique closes in chaos

JUNE
Apple Corps buys 3 Savile Row, London, at a cost of £500,000

30 AUGUST
'Hey Jude' is the first release on the Apple label

4 FEBRUAR
Lee and John Eastman are appointed as lawyers

SEPTEMBER
Neil Aspinall is appointed temporary MD

30 JANUARY
Rooftop concert at 3 Savile Row; this is the band's last live gig together

SEPTEMBER
The business moves into Apple HQ at 3 Savile Row

JANUARY
John Lennon and Yoko Ono meet Allen Klein

3 FEBRUARY
Klein is appointe The Beatles' financ representative

3 FEBRUARY
Zapple Records launches but Klein closes it down after two releases

Year

- 1967
- 1969
- 1971
- 1968
- 1970
- 1975

MARCH
Klein is no longer manager of The Beatles as a partnership, only of John, George and Ringo as individuals

Apple Corps is restructured to manage the business aspect of The Beatles' recording archive

DECEMBER
McCartney sues the other Beatles to dissolve the partnership

SEPTEMBER
Apple Studios re-opens

16 MAY
Apple Studios closes

MAY
Album and film of *Let It Be* are released

21 MARCH
Klein is appointed interim business manager

MARCH
Klein commissions Phil Spector to produce *Let It Be*

SEPTEMBER
Klein secures improved deal with Capitol

8 MAY
Klein is given a 3-year contract as business manager, closes Apple Electronics and axes half the staff. Neil Aspinall is sacked but reinstated on the group's insistence

> "IF WE DON'T MAKE ANY MONEY WHAT DOES IT F*CKING MATTER? WE 'RE NOT BUSINESS FREAKS, WE'RE ARTISTS."
>
> —John Lennon, 1967

APPLE PIE CHART

APPLE FILM

APPLE RECORDS

APPLE MUSIC PUBLISHING

APPLE STUDIO

APPLE RETAIL

APPLE ELECTRONIC

INFLUENCERS
THE
BEATLES
INFLUENCES

ROCK 'N' ROLL
ROCKABILLY
AMERICAN GIRL GROUPS
BLUES
ELVIS PRESLEY
MOTOWN
CHUCK BERRY
R&B
THE MARVELETTES
GOSPEL
SKIFF...
EVERLY BROTHERS
LITTLE RICHARD
MUSI...
COUNTRY
RAY CHARLES
BOB DYLAN
FOLK
SOUL
RAVI SHANKAR
DANCE HALL
BIG BAND
JAZZ
INDIAN CLASSICAL

As John Lennon said, "if there hadn't been an Elvis, there wouldn't have been The Beatles." This was true for many bands, but The Beatles' longevity and creativity drew from more than a single musical tradition. Being eclectics rather than purists, with ears and brains open to any and many different musical genres, they joyfully mixed in black American R&B, girl-group harmonies, music-hall songs, dance tunes and whatever else they fancied to produce a new and distinctive sound.

THE
BEATLES

03
WORK

"THEY WERE DOING THINGS NO ONE ELSE WAS DOING... EVERYBODY ELSE THOUGHT THEY WERE JUST FOR THE TEENYBOPPERS, THAT THEY WERE GONNA PASS RIGHT AWAY.

BUT IT WAS OBVIOUS TO ME THAT THEY HAD STAYING POWER. I KNEW THEY WERE POINTING THE DIRECTION THAT MUSIC HAD TO GO."

—Bob Dylan, 1971

HERE, THERE AND EVERYWHERE

1,400 PERFORMANCES IN 10 YEARS

16 COUNTRIES TOURED

CANADA
1964/65/66

200 GIGS

7

SWEDEN 5

9

176

CHANNEL ISLANDS 3

USA
1964/65/66

EIGHT DAYS A WEEK 1963

The Beatles were on and off the road from June 1962 to 29 August 1966 but the crunch year was 1963. They toured relentlessly in between making radio shows and TV programmes, writing songs and recording their second album, *With The Beatles*.

For the first half of their career, The Beatles were a full-on touring band. In their pre-Ringo days, they had rocked around Scotland as a rather indifferent backing band for Johnny Gentle and put in punishing shifts in the cellars of Hamburg. But after the huge smash of their second single 'Please Please Me' (January 1963) and the album that followed, touring really took off. As their fame spread, their itineraries expanded – they performed in 16 countries, giving over 1,400 performances. By 1966, jaded, exhausted and tired of having no time to themselves, or to pursue their own creative paths, they called it a day. The second half of the band's career would be devoted to studio work.

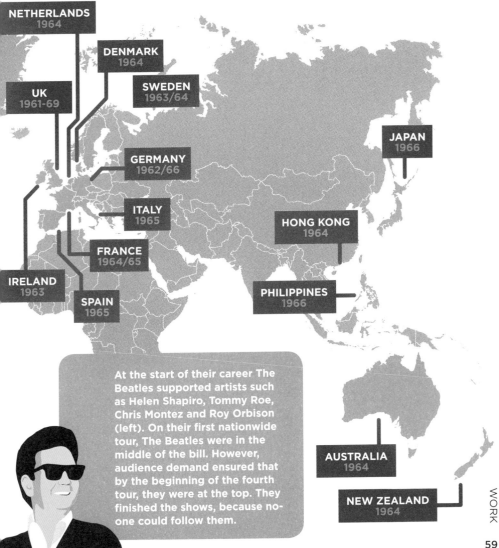

NETHERLANDS
1964

DENMARK
1964

SWEDEN
1963/64

UK
1961-69

JAPAN
1966

GERMANY
1962/66

ITALY
1965

HONG KONG
1964

FRANCE
1964/65

IRELAND
1963

SPAIN
1965

PHILIPPINES
1966

AUSTRALIA
1964

NEW ZEALAND
1964

At the start of their career The Beatles supported artists such as Helen Shapiro, Tommy Roe, Chris Montez and Roy Orbison (left). On their first nationwide tour, The Beatles were in the middle of the bill. However, audience demand ensured that by the beginning of the fourth tour, they were at the top. They finished the shows, because no-one could follow them.

WORK

ANATOMY OF AN ALBUM: RUBBER SOUL

SIDE 1

DRIVE MY CAR
The first Beatles recording session to go beyond midnight. One of the first narrative songs.

NORWEGIAN WOOD
First use of sitar on a Western pop record; the lyrics are a sly reference to an affair John had with a journalist.

YOU WON'T SEE ME
Written as Paul and Jane Asher were drifting apart.

NOWHERE MAN
The Beatles first song about something other than love. John wrote it to chronicle his feelings of despair and self-loathing.

THINK FOR YOURSELF
Features two basses.

THE WORD
Paul described it as an attempt to write a song on one note. Both Paul and John smoked extra marijuana to write this early peace and love anthem. The first Beatles "message" song.

MICHELLE
Possibly made by Paul using overdubbing in a 9-hour session. It started out as a spoof French song Paul used to sing to amuse at parties.

SIDE 2

WHAT GOES ON
Ringo's vocal contribution to the album; he also contributed to the lyrics. John had started to write it in 1963.

GIRL
John's response to Michelle; a Euro-sounding song with German and Greek embellishments.

I'M LOOKING THROUGH YOU
Written as a comment on the state of Paul's relationship with Jane Asher.

IN MY LIFE
Electric piano recorded at half speed then speeded up to sound like a harpsichord.

WAIT
First recorded for *Help!* in 1965 but not used; revamped with extra percussion.

IF I NEEDED SOMEONE
Written for Pattie Boyd, George's girlfriend, later wife; composition influenced by Indian classical music.

RUN FOR YOUR LIFE
John dismissed it as a throwaway song.

RECORDED:
October and November 1965

WRITING CREDITS

- Lennon & McCartney but mostly Lennon
- Lennon & McCartney but mostly McCartney
- Lennon & McCartney
- Harrison

RELEASED:
3 December 1965

Rubber Soul was a transitional album for the band and for pop music across the board. It was the first album over which The Beatles had total artistic control – they had unprecedented final say on the content, running order and even cover art, but more importantly they were given free rein in the studio, where they learned to create their own soundscapes. The album was a game-changer, shifting the emphasis from singles to albums as the defining platform for aspiring bands, synthesising the many strands of musical genres blowing in the wind of the era, and inspiring bands to lend to and borrow from each other. It was one of the first indications that pop music was growing up.

The album was created after The Beatles returned from their two-week tour of the US in 1965. During their time there they had met Dylan, Elvis, The Byrds, and David Crosby among others, and John, George and Paul had had their first LSD trips. Their American experiences surfaced in the songs (as well as the woozy cover art) on the album. References to folk rock, blues, country, Motown and soul can all be heard. They had learned from Dylan that song lyrics could be social observation, narrative, personal experience – relationships that go beyond the 'she loves you' stage. The influence was reciprocal. Brian Wilson of The Beach Boys called the album, "Probably the greatest record ever."

US INFLUENCES ON THE SONGS

OTIS REDDING
'DRIVE MY CAR'
SOUL

BOB DYLAN
'NORWEGIAN WOOD'
FOLK ROCK

THE FOUR TOPS
'YOU WON'T SEE ME'
MOTOWN

BOB DYLAN
'THINK FOR YOURSELF'
FOLK ROCK

JAMES BROWN
'THE WORD'
WILSON PICKETT

NINA SIMONE
'MICHELLE'
SOUL/BLUES

CHET ATKINS
'WHAT GOES ON'
COUNTRY

THE BEACH BOYS
'GIRL'
ROCK

BOB DYLAN
'IN MY LIFE'
FOLK ROCK

THE BYRDS
'IF I NEEDED SOMEONE'
ROCK

ELVIS PRESLEY
'RUN FOR YOUR LIFE'
ROCK

Rubber Soul is a pun on soul music and the rubber sole of a shoe. It is a playful riposte to "plastic soul" – a rather sniffy put-down of The Rolling Stones by an American blues singer.

RECORD BREAKERS

Liberated from the necessity of recording only material they could replicate in performance, The Beatles spent most of the second half of the 1960s in EMI's Abbey Road Studio 2. Joyfully shoving the envelope in all directions, they quickly learned how to use the studio itself as an instrument – or rather how to inspire producer George Martin to make the sounds in their heads audible to everyone else. The Beatles were the first rock band to integrate studio techniques into composition: sampling, multitracking, playing around with tape speed and direction, or using feedback as part of a song rather than something to be eliminated. Many of the effects and techniques invented and developed during The Beatles' sessions quickly became studio norms, especially ADT (automatic double tracking), invented in 1966 by Ken Townsend at John's request.

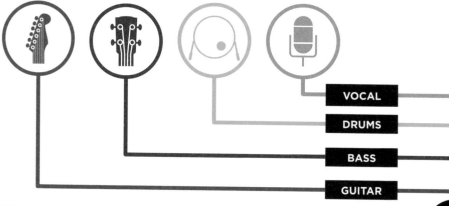

VOCAL

DRUMS

BASS

GUITAR

TECHNO REVOLUTION

Most Beatles' records were recorded on 4-track machines.

- **Multitrack devices work by simultaneously recording different audio input onto separate 'tracks' (areas of the tape) on the same reel-to-reel magnetic tape. A 4-track machine has four of these tracks.**

- **Each instrument or voice is recorded on a different track on the tape (1). The recording of each track can be simultaneous, or added at different times.**

- **Each track can be worked on without having to do the whole thing again. Tracks can be dubbed later, overdubbed, scrubbed off and replaced.**

- **Multitrack devices make reduction mixing ('bouncing') possible (2). Once the tracks have been satisfactorily mixed, they are recorded on an unused track, or on another machine. This frees up the tracks to be re-used for more effects.**

OK?

YES

GO TO PRESS

REMIX EACH OR ALL TRACKS

NO

MORE BOUNCE REQUIRED!

THIS CA
GO ON A
INFINITU

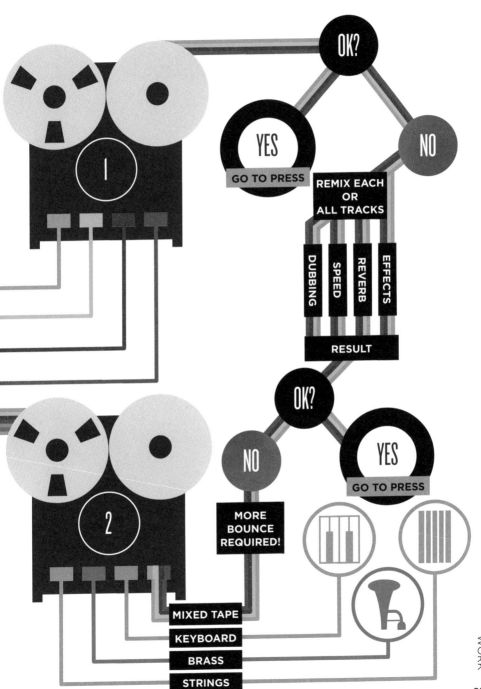

ANATOMY OF AN ALBUM: SGT. PEPPER'S LONELY HEARTS CLUB BAND

SIDE 1

SERGEANT PEPPER'S LONELY HEARTS CLUB BAND (2:02)
The character of Sergeant Pepper was conceived by Paul.

WITH A LITTLE HELP FROM MY FRIENDS (2:44)
Originally called Badfinger Boogie, because John had an injured finger when he wrote the tune.

LUCY IN THE SKY WITH DIAMONDS (3:28)
Inspired by 4-year- old Julian Lennon's drawing of his schoolfriend Lucy O' Donnell.

GETTING BETTER (2:47)
Inspired by drummer Jimmy Nicol, who subbed on a 1963 tour when Ringo fell ill. His catchphrase was "It's getting better."

FIXING A HOLE (2:36)
Wrongly thought to be about heroin; Paul says it is about marijuana and freeing your mind.

SHE'S LEAVING HOME (3:35)
The Beatles sing, but play no instruments on this track!

BEING FOR THE BENEFIT OF MR KITE! (2:37)
Inspired by a Victorian circus poster John bought in a Kentish antique shop.

SIDE 2

WITHIN YOU, WITHOUT YOU (5:05)
No other Beatles, apart from George, on this track. All musical instruments played by Indian or English session musicians.

WHEN I'M 64 (2:37)
Paul wrote this tune when he was 15 as a homage to his father and to music of the 1920s and 30s.

LOVELY RITA (2:42)
Much use of varispeeding.

GOOD MORNING, GOOD MORNING (2:41)
The animal noises were arranged in order of ability of the animal in question being able to eat or frighten its predecessor.

SERGEANT PEPPER'S LONELY HEARTS CLUB BAND REPRISE (2:16)
Neil Aspinall suggested reprising the opener in a shorter form to bookend the performance.

A DAY IN THE LIFE (5:33)
Two separate songs combined, mashed together to evoke the simultaneous existence of two states of consciousness the mundane and the transcendent.

RECORDED:
24 November 1966–21 April 1967

WRITING CREDITS	○ Lennon & McCartney but mostly Lennon	● Lennon & McCartney
	● Lennon & McCartney but mostly McCartney	● Harrison

RELEASED:
26 May 1967

This iconic piece of British psychedelia was released just in time to become the soundtrack of the Summer of Love in 1967. It was the first time a pop band had recorded an album full of material that was not intended to be performed – the album itself was the performance. Paul was its architect: it was his idea to create a band within a band, springing The Beatles from their mop-top prison and freeing up their energy and creativity – and he wrote more than half the songs. It's not really a concept album – although it inspired others. There is no thematic, narrative or stylistic link – the concept was the alter ego band and the freedom that comes from getting out of your own head.

NUMBER 1 ALBUM

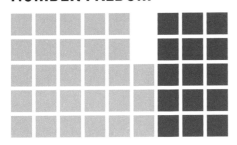

- UK for 28 weeks
- USA for 15 weeks

700hrs

Number of hours of studio time to record

5.16m COPIES SOLD IN UK

32m COPIES SOLD WORLDWIDE

The equally iconic cover was also a game changer. According to Paul, the cover concept came first – a random bunch of people gathering to applaud the band after a concert. Each Beatle made a list of his favourite icons, and pop artists Peter Blake and Jann Haworth created the crowd, sticking black and white photographs onto cardboard cut-outs and hand-colouring most of them. After Blake and Haworth's tour de force, cover art became an essential aspect of album making.

COVER FACTOIDS

- Jesus Christ, Ghandi and Hitler were considered too controversial to include. Ghandi would have been number 68 in the front row.

- Shirley Temple appears three times, twice in the line-up and once as a doll prop. No one knows why.

- It was the first album cover to print the lyrics on the back, so that the crowd could sing along.

THE ALBUMS

Before The Beatles, pop bands would go into the studio and do what they were told. Albums were essentially collections of singles. The Beatles changed all that. They were lucky to be assigned producer George Martin at Parlophone, and he was astute enough to listen to them, see their talent and help them hone and develop it. Together they changed the way pop albums were made, and established a precedent for bands to exert creative control over their own product, from content, sound and running order to cover art.

Here is The Beatles' core catalogue of 13 albums plus the three Anthology albums, which include almost every sound they ever made, including outtakes and home recordings. It does not include albums that repackaged existing material for the US, compilations, mash-ups, bootlegs or box sets.

 ALBUMS **ANTHOLOGIES**

SALES NUMBERS

	GOLD	PLATINUM
AUSTRALIA	35,000	70,000
CANADA	40,000	80,000
FRANCE	50,000	100,000
GERMANY	100,000	200,000
UK	100,000	300,000
USA	500,000	1,000,000

 Peak chart number

1963 | 1

PLEASE PLEASE ME
UK   CAN   AUS
USA

1965 | 1

HELP!
AUS
UK   USA x2   CAN x3

1968 | 1

MAGICAL MYSTERY TOUR
UK   AUS
CAN x4   USA x6

1970 | 1

LET IT BE
UK   FRA
AUS   CAN x3   USA x4

1963 · 1

WITH THE BEATLES

USA · CAN · AUS · GER · UK

1964 · 1

A HARD DAY'S NIGHT

UK · AUS · USA · CAN

1964 · 1

BEATLES FOR SALE

UK · CAN · AUS · USA

1965 · 1

RUBBER SOUL

GER · UK · AUS · CAN x2 · USA x6

1966 · 1

REVOLVER

UK · AUS · CAN x2 · USA x5

1967 · 1

SGT. PEPPER'S LONELY HEARTS CLUB BAND

FRA · GER · AUS x4 · CAN x8 · USA x11 · UK x17

1968 · 1

THE BEATLES

FRA · UK x2 · AUS x2 · CAN x8 · USA x24

1969 · 3

YELLOW SUBMARINE

UK · CAN · USA

1969 · 1

ABBEY ROAD

FRA · GER · UK x2 · AUS x3 · CAN x10 · USA x12

1995 · 2

ANTHOLOGY ONE

EUR · UK x2 · USA x8 · CAN x9

1996 · 1

ANTHOLOGY TWO

FRA · UK · USA x4 · CAN x4

1996 · 4

ANTHOLOGY THREE

UK · CAN x2 · USA x3

THE SINGLES

THE BEATLES RELEASED **63** SINGLES WORLDWIDE BETWEEN 1962 AND 1970 **24** UK ONLY

GLOBAL NUMBER ONES

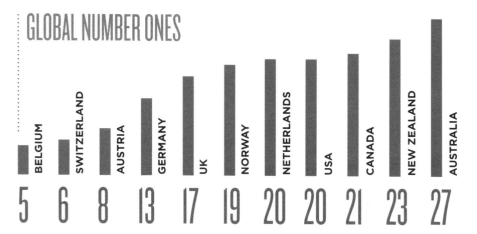

BELGIUM	SWITZERLAND	AUSTRIA	GERMANY	UK	NORWAY	NETHERLANDS	USA	CANADA	NEW ZEALAND	AUSTRALIA
5	6	8	13	17	19	20	20	21	23	27

From The Beatles' first single - 'Love Me Do', described by Ian MacDonald as, "Standing out like a bare brick wall in a suburban sitting-room" – to their last, 'Let It Be' ('The Long and Winding Road' in the US), The Beatles ruled the 1960s charts. Rapid-fire singles and EPs filled both the UK Hit Parade and the *Billboard* Hot 100. They averaged one chart topper every 14 weeks or so; that in itself is an all-time record. And we are only talking core catalogue here; that is, songs recorded during the band's working years, 1962–70. Re-releases, remixes, compilations, reformats, stuff from the vaults, cassettes, CDs, downloads or unauthorized compilations, edits and rehashes are not included.

TOP TEN BEST SELLING SINGLES

SHE LOVES YOU — 1

1.92 MILLION
copies sold as of December 2018

I WANT TO HOLD YOUR HAND — 2

CAN'T BUY ME LOVE — 3

I FEEL FINE — 4

DAY TRIPPER/WE CAN WORK IT OUT — 5

HEY JUDE — 6

HELP! — 7

FROM ME TO YOU — 8

HELLO GOODBYE — 9

GET BACK — 10

1963 FIRST UK NUMBER ONE

1969
Final number 1 in UK is 'The Ballad of John and Yoko'.

ANATOMY OF AN ALBUM: THE BEATLES

Its official name is *The Beatles,* but it is more commonly known as the *'White Album'*.

SIDE 1

BACK IN THE USSR
Ringo had temporarily left the band after arguing with Paul over a drum part.

DEAR PRUDENCE
Written in India for Prudence, sister of Mia Farrow, influenced by a guitar-picking style learned from Donovan.

GLASS ONION
Playful yet patronising meta song referencing previous work.

OB-LA-DI, OB-LA-DA
Ob-la-di Ob-la-da is a rendition of a saying from Southern Nigeria that Paul learnt from conga player Jimmy Scott. It took 42 hours to complete.

WILD HONEY PIE
Written as a singalong in Rikishesh.

THE CONTINUING STORY OF BUNGALOW BILL
Featured backing vocals by everyone in the studio including Yoko Ono and Maureen Starkey.

WHILE MY GUITAR GENTLY WEEPS
Eric Clapton plays the guitar solo. It took 37 hours and two remakes to record.

HAPPINESS IS A WARM GUN
A fusion of three Lennon song fragments, it was banned by the BBC.

SIDE 2

MARTHA MY DEAR
Martha was McCartney's pet, an Old English Sheepdog.

I'M SO TIRED
Written in India, influenced by a guitar-picking style The Beatles learned from Donovan.

BLACKBIRD
Inspired by the Civil Rights Movement in the US, which had appropriated the pejorative term 'blackbird' (a relic of the slave trade) and put a positive spin on it.

PIGGIES
Seen by mass-murderer Charles Manson as a message to kill the rich.

ROCKY RACOON
A mini, one-act Wild West opera.

DON'T PASS ME BY
Ringos' first composition, written 4 years earlier in 1963.

WHY DON'T WE DO IT IN THE ROAD
Started in India, inspired by the sight of carefree, copulating monkeys.

I WILL
Took 67 takes to record. Paul was still writing it while recording.

JULIA
A lovesong to Lennon's mother, Julia.

Written and recorded over the summer of 1968, the 'White Album' was released in November and was the band's first album for their own label, Apple. A minimalist white-on-white cover (by Richard Hamilton) sheathed a two-disc fest of self-indulgence mixed with genius. It felt as though the band members were each pursuing personal projects and using each other as session musicians. Things got bad tempered. George and Ringo left the band temporarily and Geoff Emerick, the sound engineer, walked off the job in July. George Martin was not always available, and Paul tried to drive the project but was resented by the others for pushing his own agenda. The band was coming apart. And then there was Yoko...

SIDE 3

BIRTHDAY
Written on the spot as a homage to Little Richard.

YER BLUES
A heartfelt pastiche expressing Lennon's state of mind.

MOTHER NATURE'S SON
Inspired by 'Nature Boy', a hit for Nat King Cole in 1947.

EVERYBODY'S GOT SOMETHING TO HIDE EXCEPT ME AND MY MONKEY
Initially called Come On Come On.

SEXY SADIE
John's sarcastic put-down of the Maharishi when disillusion set in. 35 hours of studio time, 52 takes, two remakes.

HELTER SKELTER
Originally 27 minutes in a single take; later revised.

LONG, LONG, LONG
Inspired by Dylan's 'Sad Eyed Lady of the Lowlands' (*Blonde on Blonde*, 1966).

SIDE 4

REVOLUTION 1
A cut-down version of 'Revolution', recorded and released as the B-side to 'Hey Jude'.

HONEY PIE
Written as an affectionate 1920s pastiche for Paul's' father.

SAVOY SHUFFLE
Written in fun about Eric Clapton's cheap chocolate habit.

CRY BABY CRY
Followed by a 28-second uncredited song by Paul, 'Can You Take Me Back'.

REVOLUTION 9
Part of the original single version of 'Revolution 1', expanded and enhanced.

GOODNIGHT
Written for Julian Lennon as a lullaby.

RECORDED: 30 May – 14 October 1968

RELEASED: 22 November 1968

WRITING CREDITS			
● Lennon & McCartney but all Lennon	● Lennon & McCartney but mostly Lennon	● Lennon	
● Lennon & McCartney but all McCartney	● Lennon & McCartney but mostly McCartney	● Harrison	● Starr

THEY'RE GONNA PUT ME IN THE MOVIES

Despite a blistering work schedule, The Beatles still found time to make movies, to a mixed reception. Only the joyful *A Hard Day's Night*, a black-and-white musical comedy directed by Dick Lester with Cinéma-vérité verve (jump cuts, hand-held camera, street locations) was a huge success at the time. The way Lester cut the film to the music prefigured the music video: today he is hailed as the father of MTV.

Help!, filmed in a haze of marijuana and self-indulgence, was less endearing. *Magical Mystery Tour*, The Beatles' own seemingly ramshackle creation, was politely panned. Individual efforts by Ringo (*The Magic Christian*) and John (*How I Won the War*, in which he first wore his iconic National Health Service glasses) did no better.

All the movies, including the animated *Yellow Submarine*, have grown in stature and are now seen as having been ahead of their time. Modern audiences are accustomed to postmodernist surreality, non sequiturs, metafiction and the anarchic breaking of the fourth wall.

Time has also been kind to *Let It Be*, a fly-on-the-wall chronicle of the troubled recording sessions of the last ever album, now seen as an essential archive. And Ron Howard's *Eight Day's A Week*, a documentary created from found footage and remastered tracks, is an unashamed love song to the greatest band there's ever been.

A HARD DAY'S NIGHT
1964

DIR: Richard Lester

RATINGS:

7.7

98%

SONGS:

Metafictional account of 36 hours in the life of The Beatles.

THE MAGIC CHRISTIAN
1969

DIR: Joseph McGrath

RATINGS:

6.1

56%

SONGS:

Episodic satire on capitalism, greed and human vanity. Ringo starred.

LET IT BE
1970

DIR: Michael Lindsay-Hogg

RATINGS:

7.8

75%

SONGS:

Fraught chronicle of the *Let It Be* recording sessions.

HELP!
1964

DIR: Richard Lester

RATINGS:

7.7

92%

SONGS:

Goofball adventure involving Ringo's ring and a murderous cult.

MAGICAL MYSTERY TOUR 1967

DIR: The Beatles

RATINGS:

6.2

62%

SONGS:

Surreal bus trip, full of absurd, ad-libbed adventures.

YELLOW SUBMARINE
1968

DIR: George Dunning

RATINGS:

7.4

97%

SONGS:

The Beatles rid Pepperland of the music-phobic Blue Meanies.

HOW I WON THE WAR
1967

DIR: Richard Lester

RATINGS:

5.8

50%

SONGS:

Surreal war movie, starring John, based on Patrick Ryan's eponymous book.

EIGHT DAYS A WEEK
2016

DIR: Ron Howard

RATINGS:

7.8

96%

SONGS:

Archive footage of The Beatles' touring years from 1962-66.

 IMDB Rotten Tomatoes

 Adventure

 Animation

 Black Comedy

 Comedy

 Documentary

 Musical

 Road Trip

WORK

WE CAN WORK IT OUT

Although The Beatles learned their trade playing covers of rock and R&B classics, their first hit ('Love Me Do') had been partially written by Paul in 1958. John added the middle eight and it was released in 1962. From then on, John and Paul wrote almost constantly, as individuals and a duo, and The Beatles forged the way for other artists to write their own material. The first all 'home-written' album was *A Hard Day's Night* (1964). Most songs are credited to Lennon & McCartney, although the contribution from each writer varies. George came late to the songwriting party but produced two number one records.

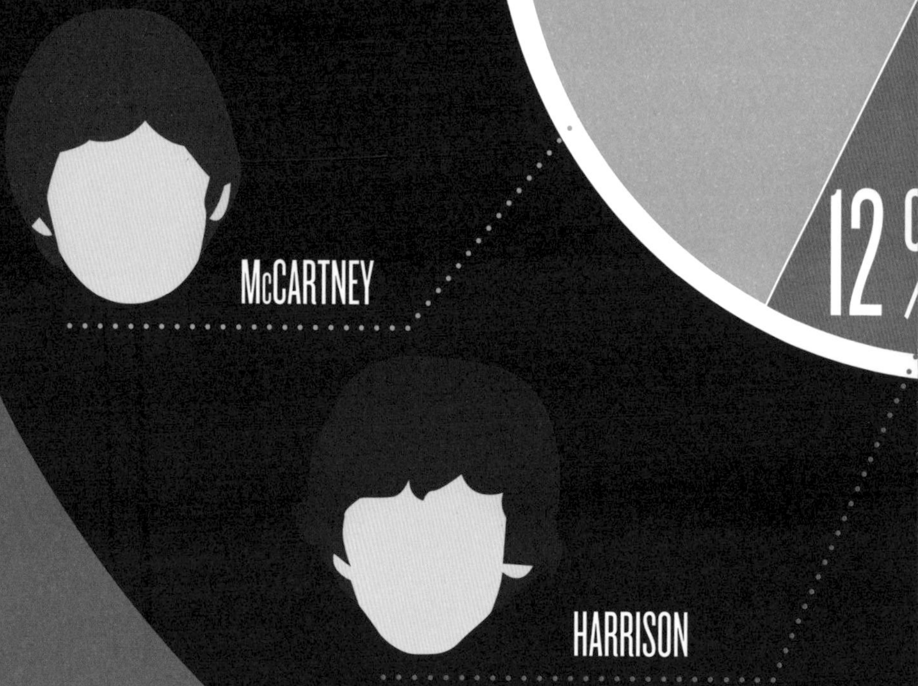

WHO
WROT
WHAT

29 %

12 %

McCARTNEY

HARRISON

LENNON AND McCARTNEY

26%

31%

LENNON

0.9%
ALL FOUR

0.1%
STARR

INSTRUMENTALS

In the studio, all the band played a variety of instruments – keyboards of all kinds, different sorts of guitar, Indian instruments, percussion – but in performance, they stuck to the traditional guitars-and-a-drumkit set-up: John on rhythm, George on lead, Paul on bass and Ringo on drums.

STANDING IN LINE

In performance, Paul always stood stage right, with John stage left. They had a microphone each, and George roamed in between, joining in with harmonies where required.

PAUL | GEORGE | JOHN

RINGO

RINGO
Ludwig drumkit and Zildjian cymbals

Ringo switched from Premier to Ludwig in 1964 and has remained brand-loyal ever since. He is left-handed, but kept the kit set up for a right-handed drummer, and so got some interesting effects.

GEORGE
Rickenbacker 360/12 (12 string)

George graduated from various Gretsches to a Gibson J-160E, but his signature guitars are the Fender Stratocaster and the 12-string electric Rickenbacker 360/12, a prototype given to him by the maker. He also played an Epiphone Casino.

PAUL
Höfner 500/1 Violin left-hand bass

A famous musical southpaw, Paul bought his iconic Höfner 500/1 Violin bass in 1963. His later favourite was a Rickenbacker 4001S, and he was the first Beatle to get an Epiphone Casino.

JOHN
Rickenbacker 325

John started with a Gibson like George's, but moved on to two alternating favourites, a Rickenbacker 325 and later an Epiphone Casino.

THE
BEATLES

04
LEGACY

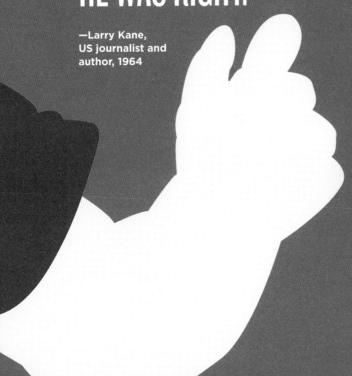

"I ASKED BRIAN EPSTEIN IN 1964 HOW LONG IT WOULD LAST. HE SAID, 'LARRY, THE CHILDREN OF THE 21ST CENTURY WILL BE LISTENING TO THE BEATLES.' HE WAS RIGHT."

—Larry Kane,
US journalist and
author, 1964

WE ALL SHINE ON

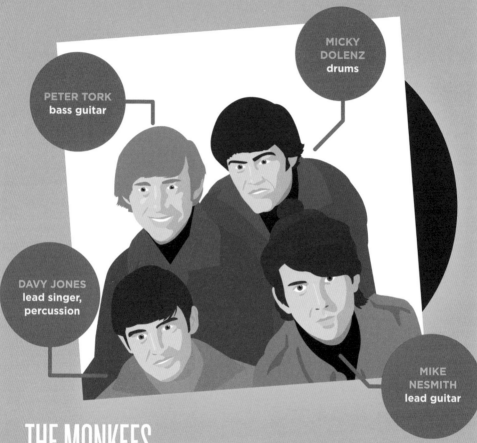

MICKY DOLENZ drums

PETER TORK bass guitar

DAVY JONES lead singer, percussion

MIKE NESMITH lead guitar

THE MONKEES

The Monkees were a manufactured band of actor-musicians, set up in 1966 for a US musical sitcom inspired by the cheeky-charmer Beatles of *A Hard Day's Night*. Gradually transforming into an actual independent rock band, complete with ego clashes and creative differences, they shed the shackles of the TV series, toured and made million-selling records (more than 75 million worldwide). They now have their own tribute bands.

GREATEST HITS

'I'M A BELIEVER'
7 weeks at no. 1, 1966–67

'DAYDREAM BELIEVER'
4 weeks at no. 1, 1967–78

When the best-loved band in the world split up, bang on the closing stroke of the decade, it really was the end of the party. A hole opened up in the world's heart, and tribute bands rushed to fill the unwelcome void with an approximation of the original joy. There are countless impeccable soundalikes all over the world, the best of which is probably The Bootleg Beatles, formed in 1980 and veterans of more than 4,000 performances. Oasis, genuinely wanting to pay tribute, were The Beatles seen in a 1990s' Mancunian mirror. Before them came two very different manufactured bands: The Monkees and The Rutles. Both started out with a different agenda, but somehow, bathed in The Beatles' afterglow, outgrew their cynical origins and morphed into creative entities in their own right.

THE RUTLES

Created in 1971 by Eric Idle and Neil Innes as a post-*Monty Python* pastiche for Idle's TV show *Rutland Weekend Television*, The Rutles went on, with slight changes of personnel, to star in the 1978 mockumentary, *All You Need is Cash*. This was a hilarious yet scathing visual and aural parody of The Beatles' trajectory, complete with Rutlemania, made with the active cooperation of George. John loved it. Innes wrote 20 songs in the style of The Beatles, 14 of which appeared on the show's soundtrack album. It was a success, the band became a reality and began to tour and record.

GREATEST HITS

'I MUST BE IN LOVE'

'CHEESE AND ONIONS'

'OUCH!'

RON NASTY
(John)
Neil Innes

BARRY WOM
(Ringo)
John Halsey

DIRK MCQUICKLY
(Paul)
Eric Idle

STIG O'HARA
(George)
Ricky Fataar

WHAT JOHN DID NEXT

So what did the chronically dissatisfied Dr Winston O'Boogie (John's joke name for himself) do next? He and Yoko Ono had married in March 1969, and had been working on projects together since 1968. By the time The Beatles officially split in 1970, Lennon's solo career was established. A move to the US, a high-profile role in political activism and the Peace Movement, persecution by the US government and varying levels of musical success followed. When his second son, Sean Ono, was born in 1975, Lennon took five years off to be a househusband, baking bread and looking after the child. In 1980, he started writing and recording again. A whole new creative direction beckoned, but Mark Chapman ended that when he shot and killed Lennon on 8 December 1980.

IMAGINE

1994 INDUCTED INTO THE ROCK AND ROLL HALL OF FAME

ACROSS THE UNIVERSE

A new V-type asteroid, 5.2km (3.2 miles) in diameter, is observed on 12 January 1983 by astronomer Brian Skiff at the Lowell Observatory in Arizona. It is named 4147 LENNON.

STRAWBERRY FIELDS

A 2.5-acre patch of land in New York's Central Park, known as Strawberry Fields, is landscaped and given a circular mosaic in 1985 as a memorial to John.

In 2001, Speke Airport in Liverpool is renamed...

LIVERPOOL JOHN LENNON AIRPORT

1969 >

Against the backdrop of the Vietnam War, John and Yoko stage a series of innovative peace protests.

BED-IN

Stay in bed to discuss peace with the world's media.

BAGISM

Hide in a bag to focus attention on their message not their appearance.

PROTEST SONG

John composes 'Give Peace a Chance', an anthem for the anti-war movement.

11 SOLO ALBUMS

SOLO ALBUMS
14
MILLION COPIES SOLD

| IN HIS OWN WRITE 1964 | A SPANIARD IN THE WORKS 1965 | SKYWRITING BY WORD OF MOUTH 1986 |

3 BOOKS

John wrote and illustrated three books which are still in print. All are collections of surreal and nonsensical short pieces influenced by Spike Milligan, The Goons, Lewis Carroll and Edward Lear.

5TH greatest singer of all time, as ranked by *Rolling Stone* magazine in 2010.

1969 John and Yoko's Bed-in For Peace takes place at the Hilton Hotel, Amsterdam.

1969 John and Yoko introduce the concept of Bagism at Vienna press conference.

1969 Second Bed-in For Peace in Montreal. Records 'Give Peace a Chance' in hotel bedroom.

1969 Returns his MBE in an anti-war protest.

1970 Releases the album *John Lennon/The Plastic Ono Band*.

1971 Moves to New York.

1971 Releases *Imagine*, which will become his most popular album.

1972 –76 FBI surveillance is conducted on the couple because of their anti-war activism.

1973 The beginning of the 'Lost Weekend', an 18-month liaison with John's ex-PA, May Pang.

1975 Son Sean Ono Lennon is born.

1975 –80 The Hiatus – John spends 5 years at home looking after Sean.

1980 Murdered outside his home, the Dakota Building in New York.

WHAT PAUL DID NEXT

What didn't he do? Barely a week after The Beatles were declared officially over, the now Industrious One had launched a solo album he had been secretly recording and was starting to get a new band together. When he wasn't making albums (about one a year), producing mega-selling singles ('Mull of Kintyre'), forming new bands, writing James Bond themes, experimenting with electronica, taking on classical commissions, directing movies, painting, supporting charities, opening the 2012 Olympics, composing video game music, setting up educational institutes and taking care of legal business, he was navigating his way through three marriages, raising a family, running a farm, collaborating with artists from every musical genre there is and getting knighted. And his touring schedule almost matches Bob Dylan's. Paul may be the richest musician in the UK ($1.2 billion to date) but he has worked very hard for the money.

1980

Arrested for cannabis possession in Japan; imprisoned, then deported.

1999 INDUCTED INTO THE ROCK AND ROLL OF FAME

ACROSS THE UNIVERSE
A new S-type asteroid, 8km (5 miles) in diameter, is observed on 11 July 1983 by astronomer Edward Bowell at the Lowell Observatory in Arizona. It is named 4148 MCCARTNEY.

MULL OF KINTYRE
2.5
MILLION COPIES SOLD

1972
Records 'Live and Let Die' for the James Bond movie of the same name.

2002
Granted a coat of arms with motto 'Ecco Cor Meum'.

1990

PLAYS TO 184,000 PEOPLE IN BRAZIL

25 SOLO ALBUMS
INCLUDING 5 CLASSICAL ALBUMS

1984
Releases *Give My Regards to Broad Street,* a film he wrote, directed and produced.

11TH greatest singer of all time, as ranked by *Rolling Stone* magazine in 2010.

1970 Releases solo album *McCartney*. Goes to no. 1 in US.

1971 Releases the album *RAM*. Daughter Stella McCartney is born.

1972 Forms new band called Wings. Records 'Live and Let Die'.

1973 Wings release *Band on the Run*, which goes triple platinum in US.

1977 Son James is born.

1981 Wings disbands.

1983 Takes up painting.

1985 Performs at Band Aid.

1989 Establishes Liverpool Institute for the Performing Arts (LIPA).

1998 Wife Linda McCartney dies from cancer.

2001 Forms nameless new band to tour *Driving Rain*; they are still touring.

2002 Marries Heather Mills.

2003 Daughter Beatrice is born.

2005 Performs at Live 8.

2008 Divorces Heather Mills.

2011 Marries Nancy Shevell.

2017 Files suit to reclaim his share of Lennon–McCartney song catalogue.

2018 Releases *Egypt Station*, which is his first album to debut at no. 1 in the US.

WHAT GEORGE DID NEXT

Without the Lennon-McCartney songwriting juggernaut to contend with, the Quiet One blossomed. He had already made two solo albums while the band were still together, and he continued to expand his musical horizons. He established his own record label, made albums, collaborated with the best of his contemporaries, and co-founded the iconic, ironic supergroup The Traveling Wilburys. Away from music, George started a movie company called HandMade Films, which produced some of the best UK cult classic movies of the 1980s. He also made generous and practical contributions to humanitarian and environmental causes, and, in 1971, set the template for the fundraising rock concert with the Concert for Bangladesh. His passion for Indian music and culture never wavered: the only Beatle to be profoundly affected by the Maharishi's teaching, he continued on the path to spirituality via Hindu philosophy and the Hare Krishna movement, and it imbued both his life and his songwriting.

2004 INDUCTED INTO THE ROCK AND ROLL HALL OF FAME

11TH greatest guitarist of all time, as ranked by *Rolling Stone* magazine in 2015.

ACROSS THE UNIVERSE
An S-type asteroid 10 km (6.2 miles) in diameter, is observed on 9 March 1984 by astronomer Brian Skiff at the Lowell Observatory in Arizona. It is named 4149 HARRISON.

RELEASES 'BANGLA DESH'
1971
POP MUSIC'S FIRST CHARITY SINGLE

40,000

people attend the concert for Bangladesh in New York's Madison Square Garden (foreshadowing Live Aid).

ALL THINGS MUST PASS
6
MILLION COPIES SOLD IN US

$12 million **Estimated relief raised from the Concert for Bangaldesh's live album and film by 1985.**

12 SOLO ALBUMS

EXECUTIVE PRODUCER ON 23 FILMS

1978–91

Sets up HandMade Films with Denis O' Brien to finance *The Life of Brian* (1979) after EMI pulls out. The company's 27 movies include *Time Bandits* and *Withnail and I*.

1970 Releases single 'My Sweet Lord', the first solo Beatle single to go to no. 1.

1970 Triple album *All Things Must Pass* goes to no. 1, outstripping McCartney's *Ram* and Lennon's *Imagine*.

1971 With Ravi Shankar, organizes the Concert For Bangladesh, the first ever megastar benefit concert.

1974 Splits with wife Pattie Boyd.

1974 Founds Dark Horse record label.

1977 Takes a sabbatical from music and follows the Formula 1 racing circuit.

1978 Son Dhani Harrison is born. Marries Olivia Arias. Founds HandMade Films.

1980 Publishes autobiography *I, Me, Mine.*

1988 Forms The Traveling Wilburys, a non-travelling supergroup, with Tom Petty, Jeff Lynne, Bob Dylan and Roy Orbison.

1994 –98 Works with George Martin on *The Beatles Anthology*, a TV documentary, set of 3 double albums and book.

1997 Diagnosed with oral cancer, but treatment is successful.

1999 Attacked by an intruder in his home, Friar Park. He loses a lung, which triggers a return of the cancer.

2001 Dies of cancer.

WHAT RINGO DID NEXT

So, what did the provider of the rock-solid backbeat that kept the band together (according to George Martin) do when it fell apart? Possibly the least ego-driven of the Fab Four, Ringo simply carried on doing what he loved: drumming. He made albums and hit singles, worked amicably (but usually separately) with the other ex-Beatles, dabbled with a record label, and made progress in his movie career – on the screen, in the editing suite and in the director's chair. After his own 'lost weekend' with the notorious Hollywood Vampires drinking club, he married actress Barbara Bach, and in 1989 formed the ever-shifting, ever-touring Ringo Starr and His All-Starr Band, still going after all these years. Together with Paul, Yoko Ono and Olivia Harrison, he controls The Beatles' financial empire. He is the richest drummer in the world, with a net worth estimated in January 2019 of $350 million.

ALL STARR BAND

2015 INDUCTED INTO THE ROCK AND ROLL HALL OF FAME

ACROSS THE UNIVERSE
A new S-type asteroid, 7km in diameter, is observed on 31 August 1984 by astronomer Brian Skiff at the Lowell Observatory in Arizona. It is named 4150 STARR.

There have been 14 line-ups. Membership is at Ringo's discretion and availability.

14TH

greatest drummer of all time, as ranked by *Rolling Stone* magazine in 2016.

THE HOLLYWOOD VAMPIRE DRINKERS CLUB

Principle members Ringo Starr, Alice Cooper, Keith Moon, Harry Nilsson.

19 SOLO ALBUMS

POSTCARDS FROM THE BOYS 2004

PHOTOGRAPH 2013

OCTOPUS'S GARDEN 2014

ANOTHER DAY IN THE LIFE 2019

4 BOOKS

1988 Ringo and Barbara attend detox clinic in Tucson, Arizona, for alcoholism.

1981 Narrates first series of children's TV show *Thomas & Friends*, featuring Thomas the Tank Engine.

1971 Releases single 'It Don't Come Easy' (co-written with George).

1971 *Blindman*, an Italian Spaghetti Western is released. Ringo plays a leading role, the start of his post-Beatles film career.

1972 T-Rex documentary, *Born to Boogie*, is released, directed by Ringo.

1973 *That'll Be The Day* is released; Ringo co-stars with singer David Essex in the story of a boy who becomes a rock star.

1975 Splits with Maureen Starkey; they had been married since 11 February 1965.

1975 Release of Ken Russell's *Lisztomania*; Ringo plays the Pope.

1980 Meets Barbara Bach on the set of *Caveman*, a slapstick comedy.

1985 Barbara Bach and Ringo marry. They split their time between London and Los Angeles.

1981 Narrates first series of children's TV show *Thomas & Friends*.

1984 Starts Ringo Starr & His All Starr Band – a super-musicians' supergroup.

1989 Inducted into the Percussive Arts Society Hall of Fame.

2002 Sets up The Lotus Foundation to support various charities.

2013 Publishes *Photograph*, a pictorial memoir with his own photographs and commentary.

2019 30th anniversary tour of Ringo Starr & His All-Starrs.

'The End', which appeared on *Abbey Road*, was the last song the band recorded collectively. It contained the much-quoted line: "And in the end, the love you take is equal to the love you make," just two of the 613 times that the word love appeared in Beatles lyrics. And in the end that was what it was all about for the band which gave us the soundtrack to the decade of love.

"WE ALL WROTE SONGS ABOUT OTHER THINGS BUT THE BASIC BEATLES MESSAGE WAS LOVE."

—Ringo Starr

LOVE YOU TO

"IT'S ALL LOVE, WHICHEVER WAY YOU LOOK AT IT, IT'S ALL LOVE."

—George Harrison

613

YOU'VE GOT TO HIDE YOUR LOVE AWAY

IT'S ONLY LOVE

ALL YOU NEED IS LOVE

ALL MY LOVING

AND I LOVE HER

LOVELY RITA

PS I LOVE YOU

SHE LOVES YOU

SHE LOVES YOU

THE NUMBER OF TIMES THE WORD LOVE APPEARED IN THE BEATLES' LYRICS

"PEACE AND LOVE ARE ETERNAL."

—John Lennon

LOVE ME DO

CAN'T BUY ME LOVE

"I'M REALLY GLAD THAT MOST OF THE SONGS DEALT WITH LOVE, PEACE AND UNDERSTANDING."

—Paul McCartney

STEP INSIDE LOVE

BIOGRAPHIES

Yoko Ono
(b. 1933)
Conceptual and performance artist, musician, peace activist and philanthropist, Ono met Lennon in 1966, and became his muse, lover and wife. She preserves the Lennon legacy, and helps run The Beatles' financial empire.

Allan Williams
(1930–2016)
Promoter and agent who launched the band when they were The Silver Beetles. He sent them on tour as Johnny Gentle's backing group, and set up their Hamburg residency with Bruno Koschmider, driving them there himself.

Brian Epstein
(1934–67)
Music entrepreneur who, as the director of his family retail empire, expanded the music and record-selling side. After seeing The Beatles at the Cavern in November 1961, he was convinced they would go far, and set about helping them to do so.

Magic Alex
(1942–2017)
Yannis Alexis Mardas, a self-styled inventor and genius with no formal training, charmed his way into the well-paid post of director of Apple Electronics. There, despite limitless funding and a wealth of ideas, nothing was ever produced.

Pete Best
(b. 1941)
Drummer and one of the Fifth Beatles, he joined the band in 1960 but was sacked in 1962. George Martin didn't rate his drumming skills, and the rest of the band felt he didn't fit their wacky profile. But fans, especially girls, protested loudly when he went.

Neil Aspinall
(1941–2008)
Trusted old schoolmate from the Liverpool Institute days, Aspinall trained as an accountant, but gave it up in 1961 to become The Beatles' roadie, and later personal assistant.

Stuart Sutcliffe (1940–62)

Artist who sold his prize-winning painting to buy a bass guitar and join the band at the persuasion of his best friend John Lennon. Stayed on in Hamburg with Astrid Kirchherr to study art, but died far too young from a cerebral haemorrhage.

Astrid Kirchherr (b. 1938)

Photographer who took many iconic shots of the band. She was a great influence on The Beatles' style and, with Klaus Voormann, expanded their cultural horizons, introducing them to modern European literature, philosophy and art.

Klaus Voormann (b. 1938)

Musician, artist and graphic designer who met The Beatles in Hamburg and moved to London in the early 1960s. He played on many of their records and designed the cover for *Revolver* and many other albums.

Mal Evans (1935–76)

Cavern Club door supervisor (bouncer), he became a roadie/driver for The Beatles, then a personal assistant and Apple Corps executive. He contributed to many of their recordings, and produced tracks by Badfinger and other Apple signees.

Maharishi Mahesh Yogi (c.1917–2008)

Born Mahesh Prasad Varma, he was a physics graduate who studied under Guru Dev. In 1955, he developed Transcendental Meditation, a form of spiritual renewal. In 1959, he toured the world with it, establishing a large network of followers.

George Martin (1926–2016)

Producer, arranger and prolific film scorer, he worked for Parlophone, part of the EMI empire, and later as an independent. Produced 30 UK no. 1 hit singles and 23 in the US. Credited with harnessing The Beatles' raw talent and energy.

- friend
- lover
- colleague
- manager
- guru
- musician

INDEX